100 Interesting Facts About Turkey

A Collection of Amazing Facts About Turkey

Introduction

Welcome to the incredible world of Turkey, a land where history, culture, and natural beauty come together in a fascinating blend! This book, "100 Amazing Facts About Turkey for Young Readers," is your passport to exploring a country that straddles two continents and has a rich tapestry of stories waiting to be discovered.

Did you know that Turkey is home to one of the world's oldest cities, a grand palace with over 400 rooms, and a unique natural wonder that looks like it's made of cotton? From the bustling streets of Istanbul to the fairy chimneys of Cappadocia, Turkey is brimming with wonders that will spark your curiosity and imagination.

So, grab your explorer's hat and dive into the magic of Turkey. Each fact is a new adventure, and there's so much to learn and love about this amazing country!

Chapter 1: Geography and Nature

- Fact 1: Unique Location

- Fact 2: Mountain Ranges

- Fact 3: Longest Coastline

- Fact 4: Rivers and Lakes

- Fact 5: Climate Diversity

Fact 1: Unique Location

Turkey is uniquely located at the crossroads of Europe and Asia, straddling two continents and connecting the East and the West. This strategic position has made it a melting pot of cultures and civilizations throughout history. The city of Istanbul is the only city in the world that spans two continents, with the Bosporus Strait dividing the European and Asian sides.

Fact 2: Mountain Ranges

Turkey is home to several significant mountain ranges, including the Taurus Mountains in the south and the Pontic Mountains in the north. The highest peak is Mount Ararat, which stands at 5,137 meters (16,854 feet) and is a dormant volcano. These mountain ranges not only provide stunning landscapes but also influence the climate and biodiversity of the regions.

Fact 3: Longest Coastline

Turkey boasts a coastline that stretches for approximately 8,000 kilometers (5,000 miles), along the Aegean, Mediterranean, and Black Seas. This extensive coastline offers a variety of beautiful beaches, cliffs, and coastal towns. The Turquoise Coast, located along the southwestern shore, is famous for its clear blue waters and ancient ruins.

Fact 4: Rivers and Lakes

Turkey has numerous rivers and lakes, the longest river being the Kızılırmak, which flows for 1,355 kilometers (842 miles). Other significant rivers include the Euphrates and Tigris, which originate in Turkey and flow into neighboring countries. Lake Van, the largest lake in Turkey, is a saline soda lake known for its unique ecosystem and stunning scenery.

Fact 5: Climate Diversity

Turkey experiences a diverse range of climates due to its varied topography and geographical location. The coastal areas have a Mediterranean climate with hot, dry summers and mild, wet winters. Inland regions experience a continental climate with more extreme temperatures, while the eastern part of the country has a more severe climate with harsh winters and hot summers. This diversity in climate supports a wide range of flora and fauna.

Chapter 2: History

- Fact 6: Ancient Civilizations

- Fact 7: The Trojan War

- Fact 8: Roman Influence

- Fact 9: Byzantine Empire

- Fact 10: The Ottoman Empire

Fact 6: Ancient Civilizations

Turkey has been home to many ancient civilizations, including the Hittites, Phrygians, Urartians, and Lycians. One of the earliest known human settlements is Göbekli Tepe, dating back to around 9600 BC. This archaeological site features some of the world's oldest known temples, providing significant insights into prehistoric human society.

Fact 7: The Trojan War

The legendary Trojan War, described in Homer's epic poems "The Iliad" and "The Odyssey," took place in what is now Turkey. The ancient city of Troy, located near the modern town of Hisarlik, has been excavated and reveals layers of historical settlement. The story of the wooden horse and the siege of Troy is one of the most famous tales from Greek mythology.

Fact 8: Roman Influence

Turkey was a vital part of the Roman Empire, with many cities flourishing under Roman rule. The ancient city of Ephesus, located in modern-day western Turkey, was one of the largest cities in the Roman Empire and is known for its well-preserved ruins, including the Library of Celsus and the Great Theatre. Roman architecture, roads, and aqueducts can still be seen throughout Turkey.

Fact 9: Byzantine Empire

After the fall of the Roman Empire, the eastern half, known as the Byzantine Empire, continued to thrive with its capital in Constantinople (modern-day Istanbul). The Byzantines left a rich legacy of art, architecture, and culture, including the famous Hagia Sophia, which served as a cathedral, mosque, and now a museum. The Byzantine period was marked by religious and cultural development.

Fact 10: The Ottoman Empire

The Ottoman Empire was one of the longest-lasting and most powerful empires in history, spanning from the late 13th century to the early 20th century. At its height, it controlled much of Southeastern Europe, Western Asia, and North Africa. The Ottomans left a lasting legacy in architecture, cuisine, and culture. The Topkapi Palace in Istanbul, once the residence of Ottoman sultans, is a testament to the empire's grandeur and influence.

Chapter 3: Culture

- Fact 11: Traditional Music

- Fact 12: Turkish Cuisine

- Fact 13: Festivals and Celebrations

- Fact 14: Handicrafts

- Fact 15: Turkish Coffee

Fact 11: Traditional Music

Traditional Turkish music is diverse, with influences from various regions and historical periods. It includes folk music, which varies by region, and classical music from the Ottoman period. Instruments commonly used in Turkish music include the saz (a stringed instrument), the ney (a type of flute), and the darbuka (a type of drum). Turkish music often features complex rhythms and scales.

Fact 12: Turkish Cuisine

Turkish cuisine is renowned for its rich flavors and variety, influenced by the diverse cultures that have existed in the region. Key elements include fresh vegetables, meats, seafood, olive oil, and a wide range of spices and herbs. Famous dishes include kebabs, mezes (appetizers), börek (savory pastries), and dolmas (stuffed vegetables). Desserts like baklava and Turkish delight are popular worldwide. Each region in Turkey has its own specialties, making Turkish cuisine incredibly diverse.

Fact 13: Festivals and Celebrations

Turkey hosts numerous festivals and celebrations throughout the year, reflecting its rich cultural heritage. Some of the most significant include the International Istanbul Film Festival, the Whirling Dervishes Festival in Konya, and the Antalya Sand Sculpture Festival. These events showcase the country's artistic, historical, and cultural traditions.

Fact 14: Handicrafts

Turkish handicrafts are renowned for their intricate designs and high quality. Traditional crafts include carpet weaving, ceramics, calligraphy, and embroidery. Turkish carpets and kilims (flat-woven rugs) are especially famous for their vibrant colors and detailed patterns. Handicrafts are an important part of Turkey's cultural heritage and are still produced using techniques passed down through generations.

Fact 15: Turkish Coffee

Turkish coffee is a significant part of the country's culture and social life. Known for its strong flavor and fine grind, Turkish coffee is prepared by boiling finely ground coffee beans with water and sugar in a special pot called a cezve. It is often served with a glass of water and a piece of Turkish delight. The tradition of Turkish coffee reflects the rich heritage and hospitality of Turkey, making it a cherished experience for both locals and visitors.

Chapter 4: Language and Literature

- Fact 16: Turkish Language

- Fact 17: Famous Authors

- Fact 18: Traditional Folktales

- Fact 19: Turkish Poetry

- Fact 20: Modern Literature whrite the facts

Fact 16: Turkish Language

The Turkish language, spoken by over 80 million people worldwide, belongs to the Turkic language family. It has evolved over centuries with influences from Arabic, Persian, and European languages. Modern Turkish is written in the Latin alphabet, following reforms by Mustafa Kemal Atatürk in the early 20th century.

Fact 17: Famous Authors

Turkey has produced many renowned authors who have contributed significantly to world literature. Notable figures include a Nobel Prize laureate known for exploring themes of history and culture in their works, and another acclaimed author celebrated for their vivid depictions of rural life in Anatolia. Their contributions have enriched global literature with unique perspectives and storytelling.

Fact 18: Traditional Folktales

Turkish culture is rich in traditional folktales passed down through generations. These tales often feature moral lessons and mythical elements, such as the legendary character Nasreddin Hodja known for his humorous anecdotes and wit. These stories reflect the values and beliefs of Turkish society.

Fact 19: Turkish Poetry

Turkish poetry has a long and rich history, dating back to the early medieval period with poets like Yunus Emre and Mevlana Rumi. Classical Turkish poetry often explores themes of love, mysticism, and nature. Modern Turkish poetry has evolved with poets like Nazım Hikmet, known for his social realism and innovative style.

Fact 20: Modern Literature

Modern Turkish literature encompasses a diverse range of genres and styles, reflecting contemporary themes and societal changes. Authors explore topics such as urbanization, identity, and political issues. Contemporary writers like Elif Shafak and Ahmet Ümit have gained international acclaim for their novels that delve into Turkish society and history.

Chapter 5: Architecture

- Fact 21: Ancient Ruins

- Fact 22: Byzantine Architecture

- Fact 23: Ottoman Palaces

- Fact 24: Modern Skyscrapers

- Fact 25: Unique Bridges

Fact 21: Ancient Ruins

Turkey is home to numerous ancient ruins, showcasing architectural marvels from civilizations such as the Hittites, Greeks, Romans, and others. Iconic sites include the Temple of Artemis in Ephesus, the ancient city of Troy, and the ruins of Hierapolis in Pamukkale, each offering insights into ancient architectural techniques and lifestyles.

Fact 22: Byzantine Architecture

The Byzantine Empire left a lasting architectural legacy in Turkey, particularly in Istanbul (formerly Constantinople). Structures like the Hagia Sophia and the Chora Church (Kariye Museum) exemplify Byzantine architecture with their domes, mosaics, and intricate decorations that blend Christian symbolism with Roman architectural elements.

Fact 23: Ottoman Palaces

The Ottoman Empire's architectural style is characterized by grand palaces and mosques throughout Turkey. Topkapi Palace in Istanbul, once the residence of Ottoman sultans, showcases opulent courtyards, pavilions, and harem quarters. Other notable palaces include Dolmabahçe Palace and Çırağan Palace, blending Ottoman and European architectural influences.

Fact 24: Modern Skyscrapers

In recent decades, Turkey's urban landscape has seen the rise of modern skyscrapers, particularly in cities like Istanbul. The Istanbul Sapphire, the Ziraat Bank Headquarters Tower, and the Isbank Tower 1 are prominent examples of modern architecture, symbolizing Turkey's economic growth and urban development.

Fact 25: Unique Bridges

Turkey features a variety of unique bridges that blend functionality with architectural beauty. The Bosporus Bridge (15 July Martyrs Bridge) and the Fatih Sultan Mehmet Bridge connect Europe and Asia across the Bosporus Strait in Istanbul, showcasing impressive engineering feats. Other notable bridges include the Golden Horn Metro Bridge and the Galata Bridge, each playing a vital role in Istanbul's transportation network and skyline.

Chapter 6: Famous Landmarks

- Fact 26: Hagia Sophia

- Fact 27: Blue Mosque

- Fact 28: Topkapi Palace

- Fact 29: Pamukkale

- Fact 30: Cappadocia whrite the facts

Fact 26: Hagia Sophia

The Hagia Sophia, originally built as a cathedral in Constantinople (Istanbul), was later converted into a mosque and is now a museum. It is renowned for its massive dome, Byzantine mosaics, and historical significance as a symbol of religious and architectural fusion. Its rich history reflects the diverse cultural and religious influences that have shaped Istanbul.

Fact 27: Blue Mosque

The Blue Mosque (Sultan Ahmed Mosque), located in Istanbul, is famous for its six minarets and exquisite blue tiles adorning its interior walls. Built during the Ottoman period, it is a masterpiece of Islamic architecture and remains an active mosque, offering daily prayers to worshippers. Its design was intended to rival that of the Hagia Sophia, symbolizing the peak of Ottoman architectural achievement.

Fact 28: Topkapi Palace

Topkapi Palace, situated in Istanbul, served as the primary residence and administrative center of the Ottoman sultans for nearly 400 years. It features lush gardens, courtyards, and pavilions housing a vast collection of treasures, artifacts, and relics from Ottoman history. Visitors can explore its extensive Harem section and Treasury, offering a glimpse into the opulent lifestyle of the Ottoman rulers and their cultural contributions.

Fact 29: Pamukkale

Pamukkale, meaning "Cotton Castle" in Turkish, is a natural wonder located in southwestern Turkey. It is famous for its terraces of travertine, formed by mineral-rich thermal waters cascading down the mountainside, creating a stunning white landscape that resembles cotton. The ancient city of Hierapolis, with its well-preserved ruins, is located nearby, offering visitors a dual experience of natural beauty and historical exploration.

Fact 30: Cappadocia

Cappadocia, located in central Turkey, is renowned for its unique landscape of fairy chimneys, rock formations, and cave dwellings carved into the soft volcanic rock. It is a popular destination for hot air balloon rides, exploring underground cities like Derinkuyu, and experiencing the region's rich history and culture. The region's surreal landscape and historical significance make it a must-visit location for travelers seeking both natural wonders and cultural experiences.

Chapter 7: Places to Visit

- Fact 31: Istanbul

- Fact 32: Ephesus

- Fact 33: Antalya

- Fact 34: Bodrum

- Fact 35: Mount Ararat

Fact 31: Istanbul

Istanbul, Turkey's largest city, is a vibrant metropolis that straddles Europe and Asia across the Bosporus Strait. Known for its rich history, Istanbul boasts landmarks like the Hagia Sophia, Topkapi Palace, and the bustling Grand Bazaar. Visitors can explore its diverse neighborhoods, enjoy a Bosporus cruise, and experience its unique blend of ancient and modern culture.

Fact 32: Ephesus

Ephesus is an ancient city located in the western part of Turkey, famous for its well-preserved Roman ruins. Highlights include the Library of Celsus, the Great Theatre, and the Temple of Artemis, one of the Seven Wonders of the Ancient World. Walking through the streets of Ephesus offers a glimpse into life during the Roman Empire. The site also features the Terrace Houses, which showcase the luxurious living quarters of the city's elite.

Fact 33: Antalya

Antalya, situated on the southwestern coast of Turkey, is known for its stunning beaches, historic old town (Kaleiçi), and vibrant harbor. The city serves as a gateway to the Turkish Riviera and offers attractions like the Antalya Museum, Hadrian's Gate, and nearby ancient ruins such as Perge and Aspendos. The region is also famous for its luxury resorts and all-inclusive hotels, making it a favorite destination for tourists.

Fact 34: Bodrum

Bodrum is a popular resort town located on the southwestern Aegean coast of Turkey. Known for its beautiful beaches, vibrant nightlife, and historical sites, Bodrum attracts visitors with landmarks like the Bodrum Castle, the Mausoleum at Halicarnassus, and the picturesque marina. It is also a hub for sailing and yachting. The town's charming whitewashed houses and bougainvillea-lined streets add to its unique coastal charm.

Fact 35: Mount Ararat

Mount Ararat, the highest peak in Turkey, is a dormant volcano located in the eastern part of the country. Standing at 5,137 meters (16,854 feet), it is famously associated with the biblical story of Noah's Ark. Mount Ararat offers challenging climbs for mountaineers and stunning views of the surrounding landscape, making it a significant natural landmark. The mountain is also a key site for scientific research and exploration due to its unique geological features.

Chapter 8: Natural Wonders

- Fact 36: Fairy Chimneys

- Fact 37: Travertines of Pamukkale

- Fact 38: Lake Van

- Fact 39: Saklikent Gorge

- Fact 40: Duden Waterfalls

Fact 36: Fairy Chimneys

The fairy chimneys of Cappadocia are unique rock formations created by centuries of erosion. These tall, thin spires of volcanic rock, some of which have been carved into homes and churches, create a surreal landscape that attracts tourists and photographers from around the world. Hot air balloon rides over the region offer spectacular views of this otherworldly terrain. Cappadocia also features ancient underground cities such as Derinkuyu and Kaymakli.

Fact 37: Travertines of Pamukkale

The travertines of Pamukkale, also known as the "Cotton Castle," are terraces of white mineral deposits created by the flow of thermal spring waters. This site offers a breathtaking natural spectacle and allows visitors to bathe in the warm, mineral-rich waters. The area also includes the ruins of the ancient city of Hierapolis. Visitors can enjoy exploring the ancient Roman theatre and the well-preserved necropolis.

Fact 38: Lake Van

Lake Van, the largest lake in Turkey, is located in the eastern part of the country. This saline soda lake is surrounded by stunning mountains and is home to the ancient Armenian Church of the Holy Cross on Akdamar Island, making it a site of both natural beauty and historical significance. The lake's unique ecosystem supports a variety of wildlife, including the endemic pearl mullet. The surrounding area also offers opportunities for hiking and exploring ancient castles such as Van Castle.

Fact 39: Saklikent Gorge

Saklikent Gorge, one of the deepest gorges in Turkey, is located in the southwestern region of the country. This natural wonder offers visitors the opportunity to hike through its cool, narrow passages, wade in its icy waters, and enjoy the stunning scenery of steep rock walls and lush vegetation. Rafting and tubing are popular activities in the gorge. There are also several restaurants along the gorge where visitors can enjoy fresh trout and traditional Turkish cuisine.

Fact 40: Duden Waterfalls

The Duden Waterfalls, located near Antalya, are a series of picturesque waterfalls formed by the Duden River. The Upper Duden Waterfalls provide a tranquil forest setting, while the Lower Duden Waterfalls dramatically cascade into the Mediterranean Sea, creating a popular spot for sightseeing and photography. Visitors can walk behind the falls for a unique perspective. There are also picnic areas and walking trails around the falls, making it a perfect spot for a family outing.

Chapter 9: Wildlife

- Fact 41: Indigenous Animals

- Fact 42: Bird Migration

- Fact 43: Marine Life

- Fact 44: National Parks

- Fact 45: Conservation Efforts

Fact 41: Indigenous Animals

Turkey is home to a wide variety of indigenous animals, including the Anatolian leopard, Turkish wild goat (ibex), and the rare Mediterranean monk seal. The diverse habitats across the country, from mountains and forests to coastal regions, support a rich array of wildlife. These species are integral to Turkey's natural ecosystem and are often the focus of conservation efforts. Visitors to Turkey can explore various nature reserves and wildlife parks to see these animals in their natural habitats.

Fact 42: The Alaska State Fair

Turkey is a crucial crossroads for bird migration, with millions of birds passing through the country every year. The Bosphorus Strait in Istanbul and the wetlands of Lake Manyas are particularly important sites, where birdwatchers can observe species such as storks, pelicans, and various birds of prey. The country hosts several bird-watching festivals, attracting enthusiasts from around the world.

Fact 43: Marine Life

The seas surrounding Turkey, including the Aegean, Mediterranean, and Black Sea, are rich in marine life. These waters are home to species such as dolphins, sea turtles, and various fish, making Turkey a popular destination for scuba diving and marine exploration. Efforts are ongoing to protect marine habitats and species, such as the loggerhead sea turtle. Marine protected areas and eco-tourism initiatives are helping to preserve these underwater ecosystems.

Fact 44: National Parks

Turkey boasts numerous national parks that protect its diverse ecosystems and wildlife. Notable parks include Mount Nemrut, known for its ancient statues and biodiversity, and Köprülü Canyon, which is famous for its scenic river and forests. These parks offer a refuge for many endangered species. Visitors can enjoy activities such as hiking, rafting, and wildlife observation in these protected areas. National parks also play a crucial role in environmental education and research.

Fact 45: Conservation Efforts

Turkey has implemented various conservation efforts to protect its natural heritage and wildlife. Organizations and government agencies work to preserve endangered species, restore habitats, and promote sustainable practices. Efforts include breeding programs for the critically endangered northern bald ibis and establishing protected areas for wildlife. Public awareness campaigns and community involvement are key components of these conservation initiatives.

Chapter 10: Famous Cities

- Fact 46: Ankara

- Fact 47: Izmir

- Fact 48: Bursa

- Fact 49: Konya

- Fact 50: Gaziantep

Fact 46: Ankara

Ankara, the capital city of Turkey, is the second-largest city in the country and serves as its political and administrative center. It is home to many government buildings, foreign embassies, and cultural institutions. Notable landmarks include Anıtkabir, the mausoleum of Mustafa Kemal Atatürk, and the Museum of Anatolian Civilizations, which houses artifacts from Turkey's rich history.

Fact 47: Izmir

Izmir, located on the western coast of Turkey, is the third-largest city and a major port. Known for its vibrant cultural scene and beautiful coastline, Izmir is a popular destination for tourists. Key attractions include the ancient city of Ephesus nearby, the bustling Kemeraltı Market, and the scenic waterfront promenade, Kordon. Izmir also hosts the annual International Izmir Festival, showcasing music, theater, and dance performances.

Fact 48: Bursa

Bursa, situated in northwestern Turkey, is renowned for its historical significance and natural beauty. As the first capital of the Ottoman Empire, it is home to many historical sites such as the Grand Mosque (Ulu Cami) and the Green Tomb (Yeşil Türbe). The city is also famous for its thermal baths, silk production, and delicious cuisine, including the famous İskender kebab. Nearby Uludağ Mountain is a popular winter sports destination.

Fact 49: Konya

Konya, located in central Turkey, is one of the oldest continuously inhabited cities and a significant center of Islamic culture. It is best known as the home of the 13th-century poet and Sufi mystic Rumi, whose mausoleum, the Mevlana Museum, attracts visitors from around the world. The city's rich history is reflected in its many mosques, madrasas, and caravanserais. Konya is also known for its traditional Turkish whirling dervishes performances.

Fact 50: Gaziantep

Gaziantep, in southeastern Turkey, is famous for its rich culinary heritage and ancient history. The city is renowned for its baklava and pistachios, making it a culinary capital of Turkey. Key attractions include the Gaziantep Zeugma Mosaic Museum, which houses one of the world's largest collections of Roman mosaics, and the ancient Gaziantep Castle. The city's vibrant bazaars offer a glimpse into its traditional crafts and local delicacies.

Chapter 11: Economy

- Fact 51: Agriculture

- Fact 52: Textile Industry

- Fact 53: Tourism Revenue

- Fact 54: Automotive Industry

- Fact 55: Technology Sector

Fact 51: Agriculture

Agriculture plays a vital role in Turkey's economy, employing a significant portion of the population and contributing to the country's GDP. Turkey is a leading producer of various agricultural products, including hazelnuts, cherries, figs, apricots, and olives. The diverse climate and fertile soil across the country support a wide range of crops and livestock farming.

Fact 52: Textile Industry

The textile and apparel industry is one of the most important sectors in Turkey's economy. Turkey is a major exporter of textiles and garments, known for producing high-quality fabrics and clothing. The country has a long tradition of textile production, with key regions such as Istanbul, Bursa, and Denizli being major hubs for textile manufacturing. The industry supports millions of jobs and drives significant export revenue.

Fact 53: Tourism Revenue

Tourism is a major contributor to Turkey's economy, attracting millions of visitors each year. The country's rich historical sites, stunning natural landscapes, and vibrant culture make it a popular destination for tourists. Key attractions include Istanbul, Cappadocia, Pamukkale, and the Mediterranean and Aegean coastlines. Tourism generates substantial revenue and supports a wide range of services and businesses.

Fact 54: Automotive Industry

The automotive industry is a key sector in Turkey's economy, with the country being one of the largest vehicle producers in Europe. Major global car manufacturers have production facilities in Turkey, including Ford, Toyota, and Hyundai. The industry also has a strong domestic component, with Turkish companies like Tofaş and Otokar producing vehicles. The automotive sector contributes significantly to exports and employment.

Fact 55: Technology Sector

Turkey's technology sector has been growing rapidly, driven by investments in research and development and a young, tech-savvy population. The country is becoming a hub for startups and innovation, particularly in areas such as software development, fintech, and e-commerce. The government is also promoting digital transformation and technological advancement to boost economic growth.

Chapter 12: Science and Innovation

- Fact 56: Historical Scientists

- Fact 57: Modern Innovations

- Fact 58: Space Research

- Fact 59: Medical Advances

- Fact 60: Renewable Energy

Fact 56: Historical Scientists

Turkey has been home to many influential scientists throughout history, including the famous mathematician and astronomer Al-Khwarizmi, whose work laid the foundation for algebra. Another notable figure is Ibn Sina (Avicenna), who made significant contributions to medicine and philosophy during the medieval Islamic Golden Age. Their pioneering work continues to influence modern science and medicine.

Fact 57: Modern Innovations

Modern Turkey continues to be a center for innovation, with advancements in technology, engineering, and various scientific fields. Turkish engineers and scientists have developed cutting-edge technologies in areas such as robotics, artificial intelligence, and biotechnology. Innovations in consumer electronics and defense industries are particularly notable. These advancements are supported by a robust network of universities and research institutions.

Fact 58: Space Research

Turkey is making strides in space research and exploration through its national space agency, the Turkish Space Agency (TUA). Established in 2018, the agency aims to enhance Turkey's capabilities in space technology, satellite production, and space exploration. Future plans include launching satellites, participating in international space missions, and developing indigenous space technology. These initiatives position Turkey as an emerging player in the global space industry.

Fact 59: Medical Advances

Turkey has made significant contributions to medical science and healthcare, particularly in areas such as organ transplantation, oncology, and genetic research. The country is known for its high-quality medical facilities and advanced treatments, attracting patients from around the world for medical tourism. Turkish researchers are also involved in developing new medical technologies and treatments. The government's support for healthcare innovation fosters continuous progress in the medical field.

Fact 60: Renewable Energy

Turkey is investing heavily in renewable energy sources to reduce its dependence on fossil fuels and promote sustainable development. The country has significant potential in solar, wind, and geothermal energy. Numerous projects are underway to harness these resources, making Turkey a leading player in the region for renewable energy production and innovation. The government's policies and initiatives support the growth of green energy infrastructure and technology.

Chapter 13: Sports and Recreation

- Fact 61: Football Popularity

- Fact 62: Traditional Sports

- Fact 63: Winter Sports

- Fact 64: Water Sports

- Fact 65: Famous Athletes

Fact 61: Football Popularity

Football is the most popular sport in Turkey, with a passionate fan base and a vibrant league system. The Turkish Süper Lig features prominent teams like Galatasaray, Fenerbahçe, and Beşiktaş. The national team has also enjoyed success on the international stage, including a third-place finish in the 2002 FIFA World Cup. Football matches are major social events, often drawing large, enthusiastic crowds.

Fact 62: Traditional Sports

Traditional sports such as oil wrestling (yağlı güreş) have deep cultural roots in Turkey. The annual Kırkpınar Oil Wrestling Festival in Edirne is one of the oldest sports events in the world, dating back over 650 years. Other traditional sports include javelin throwing (cirit) and archery, which have historical significance and are celebrated through various festivals and events. These sports are an important part of Turkey's cultural heritage and are preserved with great pride.

Fact 63: Winter Sports

Turkey offers excellent opportunities for winter sports, particularly in regions like Uludağ, Palandöken, and Erciyes. These areas have well-developed ski resorts with facilities for skiing, snowboarding, and other winter activities. Turkey has hosted several international winter sports competitions, attracting enthusiasts from around the world. The country's mountainous terrain and winter tourism infrastructure make it a top destination for winter sports lovers.

Fact 64: Water Sports

With its extensive coastlines along the Aegean, Mediterranean, and Black Seas, Turkey is a prime destination for water sports. Popular activities include sailing, windsurfing, scuba diving, and kiteboarding. Coastal cities such as Bodrum, Antalya, and Fethiye are renowned for their water sports facilities and attract both amateur and professional athletes. The warm climate and crystal-clear waters enhance the experience for water sports enthusiasts.

Fact 65: Famous Athletes

Turkey has produced many renowned athletes who have achieved international success in various sports. One legendary weightlifter was known for their remarkable strength and multiple Olympic gold medals. Other notable athletes include a basketball player who made significant contributions to their team, a footballer who gained prominence in both domestic and international leagues, and a boxer recognized for their impressive career. Their achievements have inspired a new generation of sports enthusiasts in Turkey.

Chapter 14: Education

- Fact 66: School System

- Fact 67: Universities

- Fact 68: International Students

- Fact 69: Literacy Rate

- Fact 70: Educational Programs

Fact 66: School System

Turkey's education system is structured into primary, secondary, and tertiary levels. Primary education is compulsory and free for all children aged 6 to 14. Secondary education includes both general and vocational tracks. The system is overseen by the Ministry of National Education (MEB), which regulates curriculum and standards across the country.

Fact 67: Universities

Turkey has a diverse higher education sector with numerous universities offering a wide range of programs and disciplines. Some of the oldest and most prestigious universities include Istanbul University, Ankara University, and Middle East Technical University (METU). Turkish universities attract students from around the world for their quality education and research opportunities.

Fact 68: International Students

Turkey is increasingly becoming a destination for international students seeking higher education. Many universities offer programs taught in English and actively recruit students from abroad. The government provides scholarships and supports initiatives to enhance the internationalization of Turkish universities, making it an attractive option for students globally.

Fact 69: Literacy Rate

Turkey has made significant strides in improving literacy rates over the years. As of recent data, the literacy rate stands at over 95% for both men and women. Efforts in education reform and outreach programs have contributed to this achievement, ensuring broader access to education across the country.

Fact 70: Educational Programs

Turkey offers diverse educational programs ranging from STEM (Science, Technology, Engineering, and Mathematics) fields to humanities, arts, and social sciences. Vocational training programs are also popular, preparing students for specific careers in sectors such as tourism, healthcare, and technology. The government promotes lifelong learning and continuous education through various initiatives and programs.

Chapter 15: Funny Facts About Turkey

- Fact 71: Unique Street Cats

- Fact 72: Nose Bonking Greeting

- Fact 73: Tulips Originated in Turkey

- Fact 74: Dancing Dervishes

- Fact 75: Pomegranate Smashing Tradition

Fact 71: Unique Street Cats

Turkey is famous for its street cats, especially in Istanbul. These cats are so beloved that they are considered part of the city's charm, and you'll often find them lounging in shops, cafes, and even historical sites. Many locals feed and care for these cats, and some even have dedicated Instagram accounts! There's even a popular documentary called "Kedi" that showcases the lives of Istanbul's street cats.

Fact 72: Nose Bonking Greeting

In some parts of Turkey, especially among close friends and family, people greet each other by touching noses. It's a playful and affectionate way to say hello! This gesture is often accompanied by a warm hug or a kiss on the cheek, showing the strong bonds of friendship and family. It's a unique and endearing custom that reflects the warmth and closeness of Turkish social interactions. Visitors might be surprised but quickly find it to be a charming part of Turkish culture.

Fact 73: Tulips Originated in Turkey

Although tulips are often associated with the Netherlands, they actually originated in Turkey. The country even celebrates an annual Tulip Festival in Istanbul to honor this beautiful flower. Tulips were first cultivated in the Ottoman Empire and were a symbol of wealth and prestige. The festival transforms Istanbul's parks into vibrant seas of color, drawing visitors from around the world to witness the stunning display.

Fact 74: Dancing Dervishes

Turkey is home to the Whirling Dervishes, a group known for their mesmerizing spinning dance called the Sema. This dance is part of a spiritual ceremony and is truly a sight to behold. The dervishes' flowing white robes and meditative movements create a captivating and serene atmosphere. Their spinning symbolizes the mystical journey of spiritual ascent and unity with the divine.

Fact 75: Pomegranate Smashing Tradition

In Turkey, it's a common New Year's Eve tradition to smash pomegranates on the ground to bring good luck and prosperity for the coming year. The more seeds that scatter, the more luck you'll have! Pomegranates are also a symbol of fertility and abundance in Turkish culture, making this tradition even more meaningful. Families and friends gather to celebrate, and the tradition adds a festive and joyful touch to the New Year's celebrations.

Chapter 16: Transport and Infrastructure

- Fact 76: Road Network

- Fact 77: Railways

- Fact 78: Airports

- Fact 79: Seaports

- Fact 80: Public Transportation

Fact 76: Road Network

Turkey has a well-developed road network that spans over 65,000 kilometers, connecting major cities and regions across the country. The network includes modern highways, expressways, and rural roads maintained by the General Directorate of Highways (KGM). Istanbul's Bosphorus Bridge and Ankara's ring road are notable infrastructure projects contributing to Turkey's road network.

Fact 77: Railways

Turkey's railway system plays a crucial role in transporting passengers and freight across the country. The Turkish State Railways (TCDD) manages the majority of the railway infrastructure, including high-speed train lines connecting major cities like Ankara, Istanbul, and Konya. Recent investments have focused on expanding and modernizing the railway network to enhance transportation efficiency.

Fact 78: Airports

Turkey boasts a network of international and domestic airports, with Istanbul Airport being one of the largest and busiest in the region. Other major airports include Ankara Esenboğa Airport, Antalya Airport, and İzmir Adnan Menderes Airport. These airports support both passenger and cargo flights, contributing significantly to Turkey's aviation industry and tourism sector.

Fact 79: Seaports

Turkey's strategic location between Europe and Asia positions it as a key player in maritime trade. Major seaports such as Istanbul, Izmir, Mersin, and Antalya handle a significant volume of container traffic and cruise ships. These seaports facilitate trade with Europe, the Middle East, and beyond, playing a vital role in Turkey's economy and global connectivity.

Fact 80: Public Transportation

Turkish cities offer a variety of public transportation options, including buses, metros, trams, and ferries. Istanbul's extensive public transportation network includes the metro, tramway, and ferries connecting the European and Asian sides of the city. Other cities like Ankara, Izmir, and Bursa also have well-developed public transit systems, providing efficient mobility for residents and visitors alike.

Chapter 17: Arts and Entertainment

- Fact 81: Turkish Cinema

- Fact 82: Music and Dance

- Fact 83: Visual Arts

- Fact 84: Theatre and Opera

- Fact 85: Television Industry

Fact 81: Turkish Cinema

Turkish cinema has a rich history dating back to the early 20th century, with notable directors like Yılmaz Güney and Nuri Bilge Ceylan gaining international acclaim. Turkish films explore diverse themes ranging from social issues to historical narratives, contributing to the country's cultural identity and cinematic heritage.

Fact 82: Music and Dance

Music and dance are integral parts of Turkish culture, blending traditional and contemporary influences. Turkish music includes genres such as folk, classical (Ottoman court music), and contemporary pop. Traditional dances like the folkloric "halay" and the elegant "belly dance" (oriental dance) reflect regional diversity and cultural traditions.

Fact 83: Visual Arts

Turkish visual arts encompass a wide range of styles and mediums, from ancient Anatolian artifacts to modern and contemporary artworks. Traditional arts such as miniature painting, tile-making (çini), and calligraphy continue to thrive alongside contemporary art movements. Istanbul's art galleries and museums, like the Istanbul Modern, showcase both Turkish and international artists.

Fact 84: Theatre and Opera

Turkey has a vibrant theatre scene rooted in both traditional Turkish dramas and Western theatrical traditions. Istanbul and Ankara host numerous theatres and opera houses staging a variety of productions, from classical plays to modern interpretations. Turkish opera singers and performers contribute to the country's cultural scene with performances of both local and international operas.

Fact 85: Television Industry

Turkey's television industry, known as "dizi," produces popular series (dizi) that have gained popularity both domestically and internationally. Turkish dramas, often featuring compelling storylines and high production values, have a dedicated global fanbase in the Middle East, Balkans, and beyond. The industry continues to expand with new genres and formats, influencing cultural trends and entertainment preferences.

Chapter 18: Travel Tips

- Fact 86: Best Travel Seasons

- Fact 87: Local Etiquette

- Fact 88: Currency and Budgeting

- Fact 89: Safety Tips

- Fact 90: Food and Dining

Fact 86: Best Travel Seasons

The best times to visit Turkey are during the spring (April to June) and autumn (September to November) seasons when the weather is mild, and tourist attractions are less crowded. Summers (June to August) can be hot and busy, especially in coastal areas, while winters (December to February) are colder and ideal for skiing in regions like Cappadocia and eastern Anatolia.

Fact 87: Local Etiquette

When visiting Turkey, it's important to respect local customs and traditions. Greetings are often accompanied by a handshake, and showing respect to elders is customary. Modest dress is recommended when visiting mosques or religious sites, and removing shoes before entering someone's home is a sign of respect. It's polite to accept tea or coffee when offered, as hospitality is highly valued in Turkish culture.

Fact 88: Currency and Budgeting

The official currency in Turkey is the Turkish Lira (TRY). While major credit cards are widely accepted in cities and tourist areas, it's advisable to carry some cash for smaller transactions and in rural areas. ATMs are widely available for withdrawing cash, and currency exchange offices can be found in major cities and airports. Budgeting for meals, transportation, and souvenirs can vary depending on the region and your travel style.

Fact 89: Safety Tips

Turkey is generally a safe destination for travelers, but it's advisable to exercise caution in crowded places and tourist areas, particularly in major cities. Stay informed about local news and follow government travel advisories. Be cautious of pickpocketing in crowded areas and keep your belongings secure. Respect local laws and customs to ensure a smooth and enjoyable trip.

Fact 90: Food and Dining

Turkish cuisine is diverse and delicious, offering a variety of dishes influenced by Mediterranean, Middle Eastern, and Central Asian flavors. Mezes (appetizers), kebabs, and seafood dishes are popular choices. Try traditional Turkish breakfast (kahvaltı) or indulge in street food like simit (sesame bread) and börek (savory pastry). Turkish tea (çay) and coffee (Türk kahvesi) are staples, often served with hospitality in local cafes and restaurants.

Chapter 19: Festivals and Traditions

- Fact 91: National Holidays

- Fact 92: Cultural Festivals

- Fact 93: Traditional Ceremonies

- Fact 94: Local Customs

- Fact 95: Modern Celebrations

Fact 91: National Holidays

Turkey celebrates several national holidays, including Republic Day on October 29th, commemorating the proclamation of the Republic in 1923. Other significant holidays include Children's Day (April 23rd), Youth and Sports Day (May 19th), and Victory Day (August 30th). These holidays are marked by parades, concerts, and cultural events throughout the country.

Fact 92: Cultural Festivals

Turkey hosts a variety of cultural festivals that showcase its rich heritage. The International Istanbul Film Festival, held annually in April, features international and Turkish films. The Aspendos International Opera and Ballet Festival, held in June and July at the ancient Aspendos Theatre, presents classical music and dance performances. Other festivals celebrate Turkish music, arts, and literature, attracting both local and international participants.

Fact 93: Traditional Ceremonies

Traditional ceremonies in Turkey reflect its cultural diversity and historical roots. The Whirling Dervishes Festival in Konya, held to commemorate the Sufi mystic Rumi, features mesmerizing whirling dance performances. Traditional Turkish weddings, known for their elaborate celebrations and customs, include rituals like the henna night (kına gecesi) and the groom's procession (damat gelişi). These ceremonies highlight family bonds and community traditions.

Fact 94: Local Customs

Turkish customs vary by region and reflect the country's multicultural heritage. In rural areas, hospitality and respect for guests are highly valued, with traditions like serving tea or coffee as a gesture of welcome. Turkish baths (hamams) offer a cultural experience of cleansing and relaxation, dating back centuries. Observing Ramadan, the Islamic holy month, includes fasting during daylight hours and communal prayers, demonstrating religious customs and community solidarity.

Fact 95: Modern Celebrations

Modern celebrations in Turkey blend traditional customs with contemporary trends. Urban centers like Istanbul and Ankara host New Year's Eve celebrations with fireworks displays and street parties. International Women's Day on March 8th is marked by events promoting gender equality and women's rights. Modern weddings often combine traditional rituals with modern elements, reflecting individual preferences and societal changes in Turkish culture.

Chapter 20: Future Prospects

- Fact 96: Technological Advancements

- Fact 97: Sustainable Development

- Fact 98: Educational Reforms

- Fact 99: Economic Growth

- Fact 100: Turkey's Role in the Global Community

Fact 96: Technological Advancements

Turkey is investing in technological advancements across various sectors, including artificial intelligence, biotechnology, and renewable energy. Initiatives such as Istanbul's Smart City project aim to integrate technology into urban infrastructure, enhancing efficiency and sustainability.

Fact 97: Sustainable Development

Turkey is committed to sustainable development, focusing on reducing carbon emissions, preserving natural resources, and promoting eco-friendly practices. Efforts include expanding renewable energy sources, improving waste management systems, and implementing green building standards to foster environmental sustainability.

Fact 98: Educational Reforms

Turkey is implementing educational reforms to improve the quality of education and better prepare students for the future. These reforms include updating curricula, investing in teacher training, and increasing access to technology in schools. New programs focus on enhancing critical thinking and problem-solving skills. The country is also expanding vocational training opportunities to align education with job market needs.

Fact 99: Economic Growth

Turkey's economy continues to grow, driven by diverse sectors such as manufacturing, tourism, and technology. Government policies support entrepreneurship, foreign investment, and infrastructure development to stimulate economic growth and create job opportunities across the country.

Fact 100: Turkey's Role in the Global Community

Thingvellir National Park is a place of historical and geological significance. It was the site of Iceland's first parliament, the Althing, established in 930 AD. The park is also located on the rift between the North American and Eurasian tectonic plates, featuring stunning landscapes, waterfalls, and hiking trails. Its unique geological features make it a popular destination for visitors interested in the dynamic forces shaping the Earth.

Conclusion

Congratulations, young explorers! You've journeyed through the fascinating world of Turkey and uncovered 100 amazing facts that showcase the rich history, vibrant culture, and stunning landscapes of this incredible country. From ancient ruins and bustling bazaars to delicious cuisine and unique wildlife, Turkey is truly a land of wonders.

As you close this book, remember that the adventure doesn't end here. There are countless more stories, places, and experiences waiting for you in Turkey and beyond. Keep your curiosity alive, and never stop exploring the amazing world around you.

Until our next adventure, keep discovering, keep dreaming, and keep being amazed by the incredible world we live in!

Thank you!

Printed in Dunstable, United Kingdom